Labor

Lisa DeSiro

Nixes Mate Books
Allston, Massachusetts

Copyright © 2018 Lisa DeSiro

Book design by d'Entremont
Cover photograph by Lauren Leja

All rights reserved. This book or any portion thereof may not be reproduced or used in any manner whatsoever without the express written permission of the publisher except for the use of brief quotations in a book review or scholarly journal.

Heartfelt thanks to everyone who supported me on my journey to this first book publication, in particular: the Nixes Mate team; the Tupelo Press 30/30 Project community; the Colrain Poetry Manuscript Conference community; my cohort at Lesley University and the faculty with whom I worked there (especially Teresa Cader, Rafael Campo, Steven Cramer, and Spencer Reece); my erstwhile Cambridge/Somerville writing group (Annie, Deborah, Sammy, Kelly); my Facebook poet-pals; my family and friends.

ISBN 978-0-9993971-3-8

Nixes Mate Books
POBox 1179
Allston, MA 02134
nixesmate.pub/books

Dedicated with gratitude to my first poetry professors:
Arthur Clements, Milton Kessler, Bill Knott

Contents

i Walks of Life

Sitting Meditation	3
Syllabics	4
Observations at the Park	6
The Yogini Came in Carrying a Buddha	7
At the Lost Sock Laundromat	8
Caught in the Middle	10
Andrew Square, Southie	11
9/11 Anniversary, Public Garden	12
Ask and Ye Shall Receive	14
Hawks in Harvard Square	15
Every Little Bit Helps	16
Commute	17
Staying Alive	18
Lunch Poem	19

ii Odd Jobs

Waitress	23
Cashier	24
Customer Service Representative	25
File Clerk	26
Warehouse Help	27
Warehouse & Office Assistant	28
Administrative Assistant	29
Temps	30
Receptionist	31
Barista	32
Human Resources	33
Junior Secretary	34
Secretary	35
Library Assistant	36
Author's Assistant	37
Registration Guide	38

iii Local Colors

Welcomed Home after Bidding Farewell	41
After the Marathon Bombing	42
Lockdown	43
National Public Radio	44
Boston Strong	45
Fiddle-dee-dee	46
Hashtag Millennial	47
The Reply	48
Pride Party	49
Immigrant	50
Hitting the Skids	51
Trumped-Up	52
Customs	54
Public Display of Affection	57
Notes	59
Acknowledgments	60

Labor

i

Walks of Life

Sitting Meditation
(a riddle)

suspend thinking and judgment and all that jazz
let words, ideas, images, the entire panorama
of the monkey mind with its razzmatazz
pass by, no need to be involved, see
through eyes half-shut half-open

Syllabics

The night sky:
a brush stroke.

The half moon:
a rice bowl.

My pen wants
to be Zen.

My fingers
want to be

chopsticks. I
want myself

to be a
warrior

who knows how
and why and

what to do.
This poem

wants to be
a haiku.

Observations at the Park

for a friend with an eating disorder

i. Just like ducks

Plunging heads and necks
underwater to feed, swans
stick their butts up too.

ii. Unlike us

Sparrows and squirrels
eat all day long; they never
obsess about weight.

The Yogini Came in Carrying a Buddha

Like a baby he straddled her waist,
his face pressed against her chest.
Her hands were cradling his butt
and so she couldn't shut
the door until she set
the statue down. It wasn't just
me who wondered what
she planned to do with yet
another in the studio. *You must
think I'm nuts,* she said. *Let
me reassure you: I did not
buy this one. I found him
on the sidewalk, and I thought
he looks as if he needs a home.*

At the Lost Sock Laundromat

There's an old woman
wearing slippers
and a housedress.
Kerchief tied over her head.
Her calves and ankles
are grossly swollen,
her skin tinged
sunburn red.

Dryers hum, clothes
tumble. Washing
machines agitate.

There's a young woman
hefting a plastic bag.
She rolls up her sleeves.
She's stick-figure-thin.
Her flat brown arms
reach into the garbage.
Her flat brown hair
is pinned with barrettes.

Dryers hum, clothes
tumble. Washing
machines agitate.

A can's a can, ya know?
the young woman mutters.
Don't care what they do with 'em.
What the hell... my life...
She pushes back
out the door with her sack.
Somebody dropped a sock
the old woman declares.

Dryers hum, clothes
tumble. Washing
machines agitate.

Caught in the Middle
(a riddle)

BAD THINGS HAPPEN TOO OFTEN HOW
LONG BEFORE WE STOP FIGHTING OH
AMERICA AMONG ALL YOUR PEOPLE I
COUNT TOO AND I CAN ONLY CRY OUT
KEEP TRYING SHARE SUPPORT LOVE

Andrew Square, Southie

...we should look and look...

Twice while living there, I was accosted for no reason. Nobody expects to be yelled at by a stranger. To say the least, it is upsetting. First time: I smile at a woman's children. She's furious. We're at the train station. She shouts *You got a problem?* Nobody could blame me for feeling stunned, right? I mean, who hates on a person who smiles at kids? Second time: I sit near these teenagers, make eye contact. *I'm sick of being stared at by white people* one of the girls shouts. Her friend giggles. I turn away. We might have made small talk in a different situation. What did I do except what people do while riding the subway? Am I not allowed to say it was unfair? Maybe. Fair enough. But I want a world where such incidents don't happen; where "us" versus "them" doesn't exist. Call it white privilege, but I want everybody to get along. I have hope. I have a responsibility. I have to keep looking; try to see more, speak more, turn away less.

9/11 Anniversary, Public Garden

Go ahead, enjoy this day. It is
a lovely time of year to be in Boston.

There's plenty of sun, a mild breeze, lush
lingering summery warmth even in late

afternoon. Notice how the ducks, geese,
pigeons, squirrels all attend to their normal

business. The people, too — look at them
go! — busily back and forth, treading the worn

footpaths beneath the wise old trees. A
typical ratio — locals and tourists,

students, suits and skirts, families and
couples in a flurry of activity —

talking on phones, walking dogs, shooting
photos, pushing baby strollers. And loners

sitting on benches or on the grass
reading, eating, watching the passers-by. See,

everyone is represented here —
men, women, and children; a variety

of age, race, ethnicity. Observe
the swan boat following its habitual

route, gliding in slow-motion across
the surface of the shallow pond. Now listen —

the Arlington Street church-tower bells
begin tolling. First, hymn phrases: *Ode to Joy...*

*Amazing Grace... A Mighty Fortress
is Our God...* Then: *Someone to Watch Over Me.*

Ask and Ye Shall Receive

Says this middle-aged man
wearing a Red Sox cap,
polo shirt, and cargo pants.
Rattling coins in a cup
tambourine-like, he chants
(You got to have faith,
got to have confidence)
and strolls back & forth,
footsteps keeping time
outside Boylston station
(Penny, nickel, or dime)
near Boston Common.

A voice from among
the cluster of younger
guys gathered nearby
on a bench yells *Hey!*
Hey! I will bust yo' ass!
The man says *God bless*
to those who give money
and to those without any.

Hawks in Harvard Square

I've seen them hover high, glide
above the buildings, citified,
or perch atop St. Paul's clock
tower. One time I saw a hawk

dive down to the street, pounce,
pluck a sparrow off. And once,
convinced I saw, quite close to me,
some bird-beast swoop into a tree,

I searched — greenish sunlight, twisted
branches, leaves. Nothing nested
there but shadows. Didn't matter.
Wind went rippling like dry water

through their feathers, through my hair,
through the air throughout the square.

Every Little Bit Helps
(a riddle)

I am the effort that precedes the outcome, the toil
that keeps every body busy with a plethora
of purpose, whether paid or unpaid, every job
big or small, every task on every never-ending to-do
list, working hour by day by week by year

Commute

This morning when I rode the T
a blind man sat across from me
and I couldn't help but see
him fondling a woman's free
falling hair. Obliviously
chatting with her neighbor, she
had tossed her tresses back. He,
struck, reached out. Though knee-
to-knee with him, she didn't feel his three-
fingered probe... I let them be,
simply watching with ennui...

But so did other riders. We
were all witnesses. My plea:
not guilty. No apology.

Staying Alive

Rush-hour run,
Technology Square,
July, hot already at 8:00 AM,
skin & shorts & tank top sweaty-wet,
earbuds blasting a classic Bee Gees track
from the Motivation playlist,
I pass a group of pedestrians dressed in corporate clothes,
baggage-laden, on their way to work —
some doing the cell phone zombie shuffle with heads bowed but
some looking up at me with morning faces —
and I feel a sudden urge to
lift my hand and slap them all
high five.

Lunch Poem

Wearing a sundress and walking
on a summer afternoon,
I'm a victim of drive-by gawking:
guy in a truck, window down.
Since while eating
I'd been reading
Lunch Poems, I think:
What would Mr. O'Hara say
or do? Being gay,
maybe relish
the attention; dish
out a coy "thanks";
give the guy a wink,
being frank.

ii

Odd Jobs

Waitress

There was a small shop at Tri-County Mall. An "open air" design, but indoors, just a countertop bar and a few tables. I had to wear an apron, tie back my hair. A man ordered coffee and when I poured from the pot I overflowed his cup and it spilled on his lap. That was my first and last day.

Cashier

I wanted to work at the movie theater, because of the popcorn and cute boys. Instead I got a job at the Seneca Knolls grocery because my friend and her mom worked there. We wore red smocks and plastic name tags. The cash registers were manual; we punched in numbers by hand. I was nervous about making change, making small talk, running a price check. I learned how to bag: heavier on the bottom, lighter on top.

Customer Service Representative

My best friend and I were hired by the same company. She'd pick me up in her parents' Chevy, radio blasting. We both liked ballads by Chicago. We both played in marching band. Being those kind of girls, we struggled to make our daily quotas. Cold calling, reading from a script, trying to get the person on the other end of the line to say yes. Our names never got written on the list, starred as top sellers. The greasy phones. The fake cheerfulness. The repetition. The ones who yelled or hung up. The best part of the job was the ride home. I quit first.

File Clerk

Sarge was the woman in charge. She wore tortoiseshell glasses, smoked like a fat chimney, sat enthroned on a leather chair behind a wide desk with an old rotary phone. She always had calls to make and calls to take and papers to sign and mug after mug of coffee and an ashtray full of butts. I was relegated to the windowless file room where I worked with Angie, a girl my age but a world away because her baby-daddy was a recovering drug addict. She talked about him and her kid non-stop. The hours went by in a haze of cigarette and carbon copy fumes: Sarge barking orders; Angie sadly chattering; me alphabetizing piles of ink-stained invoices, filing them in deep drawers of tall metal cabinets heavy enough to crush someone if they ever fell over.

Warehouse Help

I liked the name of the company: Traffic Control Technologies. They manufactured signal lights and road signs. We were a seasonal group hired to take inventory: tallying with calculators, filling out forms with ballpoint pens. Metal shelves from floor to ceiling, everything on them sharp-edged and heavy. There was a metal box screwed to one wall, where we inserted cardboard time cards. Punching in. Punching out. I liked that we could wear jeans and sneakers.

Warehouse & Office Assistant

In the office I did data entry, my fingers fast and accurate on the keypads. Or I helped with mass mailings, stuffing stacks of envelopes with letters crisply folded by the fancy copy machine. But I spent most of my time in the warehouse, where I made myself one of the guys. They were a three-person crew. Tommy ran the show — a short man of 60 or so, wiry, spry as an elf. He always said *Gesundheit* when someone sneezed. And then Joel would say *The first time!* and snicker. Joel the goofball with his long curly hair and glasses, in his late 20s, a few years older than me. *Pee right back* he'd say every time he took a bathroom break. Lou was the quiet one, heavyset, with a walrus mustache. He'd say *young lady* in a fatherly way. They teased me for calling the box cutter a "slicer" but it impressed them that I could operate the fork lift and carry a 50-pound box. I reorganized the entire stocking system, neatly arranged in labeled containers on the shelves. The president gave each female employee a bottle of perfume at Christmas; the men got bottles of port. The women arranged my farewell party: a card signed by everyone, a blue-frosted sheet cake, and a laundry basket filled with useful stuff for a college student. I blushed at the packages of condoms.

Administrative Assistant

I joined the President's Office staff, working with two other women: Lauren (a Jewish writer) and Karen (an African-American singer). Both were strong, smart, older and wiser than me. We had things in common, had fun together, got shit done (most of it unacknowledged). I worked half-days; sorted the mail, organized the filing system, answered the phone, assisted with projects and special events. (At one, I helped Natalie Cole put on her coat.) We were required to put our initials at the bottom of the page whenever we typed letters dictated by the president. A letter I typed (printed as usual on the official college letterhead) wound up framed and hanging near the stage at Wally's.

Temps

My office mate was from India. Every day he wore the same leather belt cinched to the last hole, and every day he wore the same cardigan. He was the thinnest man I'd ever seen, almost as skinny as me. We were both always cold, sitting for hours in that air-conditioned room. We were being paid minimum wage to do minimum work. We were transitional, filling positions soon to be dissolved. Filing the few papers that arrived in the mail. Answering the phones on the few occasions when they rang. For lunch, he drank Ensure. He lined up the empty cans in a row across his desk. He had hair like a snug-fitting cap, delicate ears, perpetual dark smudges under his eyes. One afternoon, out of nowhere he said, in his low lilting voice: *I wish an elephant would pass by the window.*

Receptionist

We were a team of nine. The director, skinny red-haired Pam. The assistant director, Joanie, a local with an accent. Her assistant Jenn, a laid-back lesbian. Four financial aid counselors: Sue, the oldest; Raquel, the prettiest; Trish, who dressed the best; Jeff, the only man. Two receptionists: Maria from Sweden and me. The pair of us shared a desk space, seated back-to-back, answering phones and handing out pamphlets and forms. We plugged in space heaters under our chairs because the office was constantly chilled, A/C running nonstop. So many callers were irate parents, confused students, all stressed out about money. I could relate. I hated greeting the people who came for appointments or came to complain. It was a full-time salaried job, with benefits. I lasted a year.

Barista

Peet's Coffee hired me despite my complete lack of experience. I read the binder full of company information: philosophy, policy, procedure. I endured the training about how to brew espresso and foam milk. I felt intimidated by the squat, shiny, sputtering machine. I worried about getting orders right, mixing up cappuccinos and lattes. This was in Brookline, where I was living in a tiny room in a cramped apartment I shared with a couple, struggling musicians like me. But the neighborhood was mainly wealthy, largely Jewish, and one day my former boss came in with his wife. I smiled while serving them, humiliated.

Human Resources

Working at the Necco factory on Mass Ave was like going back in time. The factory workers (mostly immigrants, mostly Hispanic) had to enter the building through a separate door. I assisted a middle-aged white female secretary who wore high heels and had painted nails and spoke with a phone voice. She fawned over the middle-aged white male boss. He blustered, self-important and condescending. I felt certain he kept a cut-glass tumbler of scotch on a tray in his office. When the factory workers came to see the secretary about an HR concern (wearing their work boots and hairnets, standing awkwardly in front of her desk beneath the buzzing fluorescent lights) she yelled at them as if they were children. I observed, mute, taking a message or typing an envelope. After that I couldn't eat Necco wafers, even though I'd liked them when I was a kid (especially the light brown chocolate-flavor ones).

Junior Secretary

My first day I was reprimanded for not wearing nylons. Regardless that it was summer, stockings were part of the dress code, along with: closed-toe shoes, skirts no shorter than knee-length, blouses with sleeves, minimal jewelry; blazers preferable to cardigans; pants allowed but not encouraged. The same rules applied to the students, who were 99% female. They took classes in typing, book-keeping, office etiquette, management skills. This was the 1990s. I greeted visitors, sorted mail, answered the phone (*Good morning/Good afternoon, Burdett School, how may I help you?*) and jotted messages on a pink While You Were Out notepad. My supervisor was a Latina woman named Nicole who appeared middle-aged because of her gray and navy-blue suits, her hair in a tight spinsterish bun. Turns out she was younger than me. I couldn't understand how she took the business seriously – until I found out she was a single mother of two, both boys.

Secretary

Filling in for a woman who, after twenty years, retired without advance notice. She'd been the executive secretary to four real estate lawyers: the senior, a gray-haired white man with a wrinkled but kind face; and his juniors, all men — one black, one Asian, one gay. I pondered diversity during my idle moments, of which there were many. Other than typing forms, taking messages, and delivering mail, there was nothing for me to do. I'd read the extra copy of *The Wall Street Journal* cover to cover. I wore pencil skirts paired with sleeveless blouses, a blazer I could take off when sitting outside during lunch. I'd find a sunny spot by the fountain, warm myself and watch the people, gaze at the panorama: busy Boylston Street, the BPL, the Marriott, Trinity church, the John Hancock tower. The office was on the 52nd floor of that building. On clear days it gave me a thrill to look out the infamous windows. On rainy days it was like being suspended within a cloud. I worked there three months, the whole summer. I even had an ID tag with my name and photo. Then they found a permanent replacement.

Library Assistant

Not at the main branch — that venerable edifice with its welcoming steps and statues, its hallowed painted entrance hall, its high-ceilinged rooms, its charming courtyard, its organized aisles of books. No, I was assigned to the Sullivan Square storage facility, near the Orange Line. A musty garage-like room where every surface was covered in dust. We were a small crew, mostly college students. Our job was simply to shelve, in order by call-number label. Even the odor of books, which I usually loved, couldn't make up for the mind-numbing monotony. I had flashbacks to learning the Dewey Decimal system. It was the middle of summer. The facility wasn't air-conditioned. We were allowed to wear shorts and t-shirts, encouraged to drink lots of water. One morning I vomited into a garbage bin the banana I'd eaten for breakfast. A few times they sent us all home because the temperature reached a level considered unsafe. City-employee regulations.

Author's Assistant

She was writing a book. I was hired to help her prepare the manuscript: formatting files, typing her handwritten notes and corrections, copy editing, indexing. I went to her house and worked on her computer. She played recordings of Gregorian chant and served me tea. The book was about finding balance. Self-help. Geared toward women. I bought a copy but never finished reading it.

Registration Guide

It was only a two-week assignment, during August, at B.U. Helping students who needed IDs. Basement room, no windows, a row of registration "agents" seated at tables, and a roped-off section for students waiting in line. Our job as "guides" was simple: show the students where to go. Ask them a few questions (*Freshman? Which semester?*) then direct them to a corresponding agent. We weren't allowed to sit down, even during brief lulls when the room emptied out. The only perk was cafeteria access with a meal card: salad bar, hot food stations, sandwiches, sushi. I ate lunch there every afternoon, hating the hours before and after. I had three college degrees. I wanted to scream each time our supervisor (a middle-aged man on a power trip) repeated *Remember you have to stand, it makes an impression.* One time when he left the room I muttered to my fellow guides: *That bastard thinks he's a big shot but his shit stinks just like everyone else.* Then I sat in the nearest chair.

… iii

Local Colors

Welcomed Home after Bidding Farewell
(a riddle)

I took the money and left and every step
I took led me farther away from all I'd held dear
I took chances, so many places to go
I took my time, squandered
took everything in stride, pro or anti
took advantage until I fell so low even a humble pig
took pity on me; then I decided, no more drama
took myself to task, headed back, grateful

I'm taken in my father's arms and he forgives
I'm taken by surprise but humbled too
I was taken for dead but now I live again

After the Marathon Bombing
April 2013

What shall we do with the stillness, do with the hate and the pity?
What shall we do with the love? What shall we do with the grief?

Carry them with us like stones as we move through our days,
taking them everywhere, holding them close to us in our city;
offering prayers and laments, giving the heroes our praise?
What shall we do with the stillness, do with the hate and the pity?

All of us in this together, human, we each want the same things:
happiness and peace; freedom from sorrow; relief;
knowing our families are safe from the dangers life brings.
What shall we do with the love? What shall we do with the grief?

Lockdown

Shelter in place. Stay where you are.
Everything closed. Nothing running.
SWAT teams going door to door.
Kept inside while they keep hunting.
Everything closed. Nothing running.
Texting and e-mailing *(I'm OK)*
while police and FBI keep hunting.
Those men lived just a block away
from me. (I'm really not OK
with this.) In fear the city waits.
Sounds coming from a block away:
sirens, helicopters. Updates
with fear in voices while we wait.
Twitter feeds and Facebook posts.
Helicopters, sirens. Up-to-date
breaking news. The lives lost
posted: faces, names. It feeds
the teeming anger door-to-door.
Heart-breaking news of more lives lost.
Shelter in place. Stay where you are.

National Public Radio

Ugly as homemade sin, she said.
I heard it on the morning show
and thought how true, some folks are bred
ugly as homemade sin. She said
may God have mercy on the dead
and spare us all so we won't grow
ugly as homemade sin. She said
it. I heard mourning on the show.

Boston Strong

as if it was any normal April day
        I took the #1 bus across the Charles River
and sat by a Conservatory student on her way to opera rehearsal
chatting with an MIT student on his way to Symphony Hall
as if it was any normal April day
        Newbury Street swarmed with pedestrians
and I dodged my way through the many meanderers
forcing myself not to look beyond lines of yellow police tape
as if it was any normal April day
        I met my friends at the tapas restaurant
and we ate and drank and cried sharing news swapping stories
smiling wait-staff bringing bountiful food to our table
as if it was any normal April day
        we headed together for the T
but we couldn't cross through to Boylston Street for several blocks
stopped by cops posted at every corner where people were
taking photos

Colored-chalk messages on the sidewalk:
WE LOVE YOU. BOSTON STRONG.
Bouquets on the barricades.
Hand-drawn posters. One said: *Bach, not bombs.*

Fiddle-dee-dee
(a riddle)

I fly the confederate flag
I'm a classic with a female anti-hero
I depict an awful battle hard won
Many love me and others can't stand me

One of my themes has to do with the law
of the land; the literati
like to analyze what I represent
I stir up issues about history, race, and wealth

I make some people upset
I make some people laugh
I show what some don't want to see

I was the most spectacular thing they ever saw
in 1939; the paparazzi
immortalized those women and men
who brought me to life word by word

Hashtag Millennial

At night the sky was white and full of crows
instead of stars and each beak offered a shiny prize.
They goaded:
Buy a scratch ticket. Can't win if you don't play.
Those lucky enough to pluck one
turned into loons and flew underwater.
We carried buckets bare-knuckled,
sanitized our hands.
Before masturbating we turned the family photos
face-down on the bureau.
They urged:
Reduce. Reuse. Recycle.
The weather kept getting weirder until
the seasons got scrambled.
We were all thumbs on our dumb phones
texting everything verbatim.
LOL OMG WTF TTYS
They twittered:
This event occurs in the past.
Replies are no longer required.

The Reply
in memory of Michael N.

We went with our mutual friend once
to hear music of the Renaissance
at St. John's church. We sat in back,
outside the confines of the black
wrought-iron caging the sanctuary.
Jesus, the saints and angels, Mary —
frozen in their rainbow glass —
seemed (to me) to pardon us
for being late, and ogling
the young monks, and giggling.

I dreamt last night you were a guest
at Easter brunch. I asked your ghost:
What do you think of death and such?
The reply, per usual: *Not so much.*

Pride Party

the Aging Bisexual insists his ass is still tight and invites everyone to touch it
the Military Gentleman takes off his shirt and explains his tattoo and weeps
the Lesbian Artist describes the found objects used for her installations
the Fabulous Host kisses guests both male and female on the lips
the Funny Guy imitates his mother's Boston Irish brogue
the Drag Queen hands out cocktails and condoms
the Straight Girl mingles and listens and thinks
no one can tame these lions roaring
laughter spilling drinks filling
bodies dancing music
playing loud and
proud

Immigrant
for Anastasia

One of my first childhood memories:
watching the pigs be slaughtered.
We were poor, in my country.
We ate everything, even the feet.

Now I live here, making money
enough to treat myself sometimes.
Today I tried a kanga burger.
It was tasty, tasty, tasty!

But, I know. Poor kangaroo.

Hitting the Skids
(a riddle)

I'm the way of maintaining good
relations, getting nations to say hi
to one another, getting people to stop
fighting, and I'm the skill
of conducting negotiations with no
hard feelings, diffusing any alarm
without causing any drama
even when handling affairs ad hoc
I'm the means of not arousing hostility

Trumped-Up
December 2015

What will suffice for Mr. Trump? Banning us all?
Him and his hair stump-speechifying us all?

Candidates clamor for our attention in the kitchen.
They're cooking holiday rump roast for us all.

A river of tears has flooded the world's basement;
there isn't a pump big enough for us all.

Pharmaceutical companies tell us not to worry,
they're making a mumps vaccine for us all.

A man, a woman, a child — whoever we are
terrorists don't care. They lump us all

together as The Enemy. We do the same.
At night the monsters jump us. All

our neighborhoods are watching. Some say
the government just wants to hump us all.

Some, for comfort, quote the famous words
of Forrest Gump: box of chocolates for us all.

Poor old Lady Liberty, trying to keep her torch
bright and not become a frump. For us all,

that light's supposed to shine. Isn't it? Unless
aliens arrive, take over, dump us all

off the planet. Or zombies. Or vampires.
Who you calling a chump? Us, all

of us are complicit. Myself included.
It's gonna be a bumpy ride for us all.

Customs

The metaphor is of plowing, of "turning" from one line to another (vertere = "to turn")...

Strange dance-like procession, this
shuffling back and forth between
stanchions and stretched barrier belts,
our bodies a moving multitude

> *verse*, noun: line of poetry
>   from Anglo-French and Old French *vers*
>   from Latin *versus* "turned toward or against"
> *versus*, preposition: action of one party against another
>   from past participle of *vertere* "to turn"
>   from Proto-Indo-European **wert-* "to turn, wind"

as if we were letters and words
the eyes follow, text turning
then returning in the opposite
direction, our order reversed.

We are a collection of truly diverse
faces, figures, shapes, sizes;
those in closest proximity become
familiar upon repeated passing

> handsome black man wearing a cashmere sweater
> > (he must be gay)
> petite Asian girls wearing glasses and backpacks
> > (they must be students)
> slim young woman wearing a hijab and jeans
> > (she must be Muslim)
> tall blond teenaged boy with tattoos and piercings
> > (he must be a punk)
> middle-aged white obese husband & wife
> > (they must be Republicans)
> dark-haired-dark-eyed family, mother & father & kids
> > (they must be Hispanic)

and who's to say it isn't perverse
that we can't stop observing because
it's in our nature, human nature,
speculating, making assumptions.

Officials, uniformed, guide us,
pointing the way. We are questioned,
searched, scanned. Stamped approval
for some. Those allowed to emerge

> cf. Old English *weorthan* "to befall";
> *wyrd* "fate, destiny";
> literally "what befalls one"

enter the terminal greeted by crowds,
cheers, banners, balloons,
a cluster of lawyers,
a pair of police officers watching.

Public Display of Affection

this couple gets on the bus
larger than life

as if stuffed full of love
they stride down the aisle

him watching her behind from behind
blue jeans hugging her hips

their bodies snuggle together in the seat
in front of mine

they are not the same color as
me or that person I didn't vote for

who said people from where they are from
are rapists and should be walled out

the man holds a cell phone wedged
between shoulder and ear

while he chatters in Spanish
the woman peers at his forehead

then presses his brow
with her ruby thumbnails

liberating a pearl of pus
they gurgle with laughter

he strokes her lustrous hair
kisses her disregarding

the large mole like a dollop of
chocolate on her lip

and I want everyone to stand up
for them and cheer

Notes

"Andrew Square, Southie" is a golden shovel that borrows phrases from Gwendolyn Brooks' poem "Beverly Hills, Chicago."

"Lunch Poem" makes reference to Frank O'Hara.

The refrain (lines 1–2) in "After the Boston Marathon Bombing" is from "For Victor Jara" by Miller Willams.

All of the riddle poems are acrostics and can be solved by reading vertically.

Acknowledgments

I'm grateful to the editors of the following publications, where these poems (sometimes in earlier versions or with different titles) first appeared.

Commonthought Magazine: Hawks in Harvard Square
Friends Journal: After the Marathon Bombing
Indolent Books (What Rough Beast): Customs, Hashtag Millennial
Mezzo Cammin: Syllabics
Pre-existing Poems: Observations at the Park
Prodigal's Chair: Ask And Ye Shall Receive, Lockdown
Rat's Ass Review (Such an Ugly Time): Immigrant, Public Display of Affection
Rattle (Poets Respond): Trumped-Up
Writers Resist: Pride Party

"Hawks in Harvard Square" is also published in the anthology *Thirty Days: The Best of the Tupelo Press 30/30 Project's First Year* (Tupelo Press, 2015).

"Boston Strong" (an earlier version with a different title) is featured in the digital archive Our Marathon: a Community Project Hosted at Northeastern University.

About the Author

Lisa DeSiro is the author of an e-chapbook, *Grief Dreams* (White Knuckle Press, 2017) and she is featured in *Nasty Women Poets: An Unapologetic Anthology of Subversive Verse* (Lost Horse Press, 2017). Her poem "In Lieu of Flowers" was a winner in the 2017 Sidewalk Poetry Contest and is imprinted on a sidewalk in the city of Cambridge, Massachusetts. Other poems of hers have appeared in various journals such as *Cordella Magazine, The Hampden-Sydney Poetry Review, The Healing Muse, Jam Tarts Magazine, Nixes Mate Review, Ocean State Review, Salamander, Shooter Literary Magazine,* and *Sixfold.* Her poetry can be heard in musical settings on the albums *Currents* and *Living in Light.* Along with her MFA in Creative Writing from Lesley University, she has degrees from Binghamton University, Boston Conservatory, and Longy School of Music; she also studied at Emerson College. She is employed as Production & Editorial Assistant for *C.P.E. Bach: The Complete Works,* and she is an assistant editor for Indolent Books. In her previous career she earned her living as a pianist, teacher, and administrator. Originally from Baldwinsville, NY, she's been a resident of Boston/Greater Boston since 1993.

Nixes Mate Books features small-batch artisanal literature, created by writers that use all 26 letters of the alphabet and then some, honing their craft the time-honored way: one line at a time.

Other or Forthcoming Nixes Mate titles:

WE ARE PROCESSION, SEISMOGRAPH | Devon Balwit
ON BROAD SOUND | Rusty Barnes
JESUS IN THE GHOST ROOM | Rusty Barnes
CAPP ROAD | Matt Borczon
HE WAS A GOOD FATHER | Mark Borczon
THE WILLOW HOWL | Lisa Brognano
A WORLD WHERE | Paul Brookes
SHE NEEDS THAT EDGE | Paul Brookes
SQUALL LINE ON THE HORIZON | Pris Campbell
MY SOUTHERN CHILDHOOD | Pris Campbell
A FIRE WITHOUT LIGHT | Darren C. Demaree
KINKY KEEPS THE HOUSE CLEAN | Mari Deweese
TEMPTATION OF WOOD | Nancy Byrne Iannucci
AIR & OTHER STORIES | Lauren Leja
HITCHHIKING BEATITUDES | Michael McInnis
SMOKEY OF THE MIGRAINES | Michael McInnis
THE LIVES OF ATOMS | Lee Okan
LUBBOCK ELECTRIC | Anne Elezabeth Pluto
STARLAND | Jessica Purdy
WAITING FOR AN ANSWER | Heather Sullivan
COMES TO THIS | Jeff Weddle
HEART OF THE BROKEN WORLD | Jeff Weddle
NIXES MATE REVIEW ANTHOLOGY 2016/17

nixesmate.pub/books

www.ingramcontent.com/pod-product-compliance
Lightning Source LLC
Chambersburg PA
CBHW070439010526
44118CB00014B/2113